가장
알기 쉽게
배우는

초등

400여 개
필수 단어와
200여 개
기본문장 수록

이지영어

STEP BY STEP BOOK 2(문형)

가장 알기 쉽게 배우는

초등 이지 영어

STEP BY STEP BOOK 2(문형)

저 자 방정인
발행인 고본화
발 행 반석출판사
2020년 3월 20일 초판 1쇄 인쇄
2020년 3월 25일 초판 1쇄 발행
홈페이지 www.bansok.co.kr
이메일 bansok@bansok.co.kr
블로그 blog.naver.com/bansokbooks

07547 서울시 강서구 양천로 583. B동 1007호
(서울시 강서구 염창동 240-21번지 우림블루나인 비즈니스센터 B동 1007호)
대표전화 02) 2093-3399 **팩 스** 02) 2093-3393
출 판 부 02) 2093-3395 **영업부** 02) 2093-3396
등록번호 제315-2008-000033호

ISBN 978-89-7172-915-1 (63740)

반석출판사
Bansok

머리말

국제화 시대를 맞아 외국어 교육의 필요성은 날로 증대되고 있습니다. 특히 영어 교육의 중요성이 강조되고 있는 현실입니다.

13세 이전의 초등학교 때가 외국어를 쉽게 익힐 수 있는 가장 이상적인 시기입니다. 그 이유는 LAD(Language Acquisition Device) 라고 하는 대뇌 특수언어습득장치가 13세 이전의 모든 어린이들에게 있기 때문입니다. 따라서 조기 영어교육의 필요성은 아무리 강조하여도 지나치지 않습니다. 조기 영어교육의 성패는 올바른 영어교육 프로그램의 선택에 달려 있다고 볼 수 있습니다.

『초등 이지 영어 STEP BY STEP BOOK 1』(입문)은 영어를 처음 시작하는 어린이를 위한 입문편으로, 영어단어 200여 개와 기본문장을 그림과 함께 편집하였습니다.

『초등 이지 영어 STEP BY STEP BOOK 2』(문형)는 제 1권에서 배운 문장을 기본으로 하여, 더 많은 400여 개의 단어와, 기본문장 200여 개로 확장, 활용할 수 있도록 문형을 중점으로 편집하였습니다.

『초등 이지 영어 STEP BY STEP』 시리즈는 모든 문장을 그림과 함께 편집함으로써, 영어단어와 영어문장을 영상으로 기억할 수 있도록 저술하였습니다. 『초등 이지 영어 STEP BY STEP』 은 특히 강의하기에 알맞도록 편집하였습니다.

『초등 이지 영어 STEP BY STEP』 이 초등학교의 영어교육에 밑거름이 되기를 바라는 바입니다.

저자 방 정 인

목 차

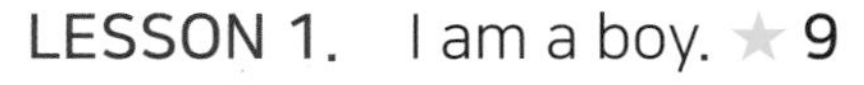

알파벳 쓰기

A a	A a
B b	B b
C c	C c
D d	D d
E e	E e
F f	F f
G g	G g
H h	H h

I i	I i
J j	J j
K k	K k
L l	L l
M m	M m
N n	N n
O o	O o
P p	P p
Q q	Q q

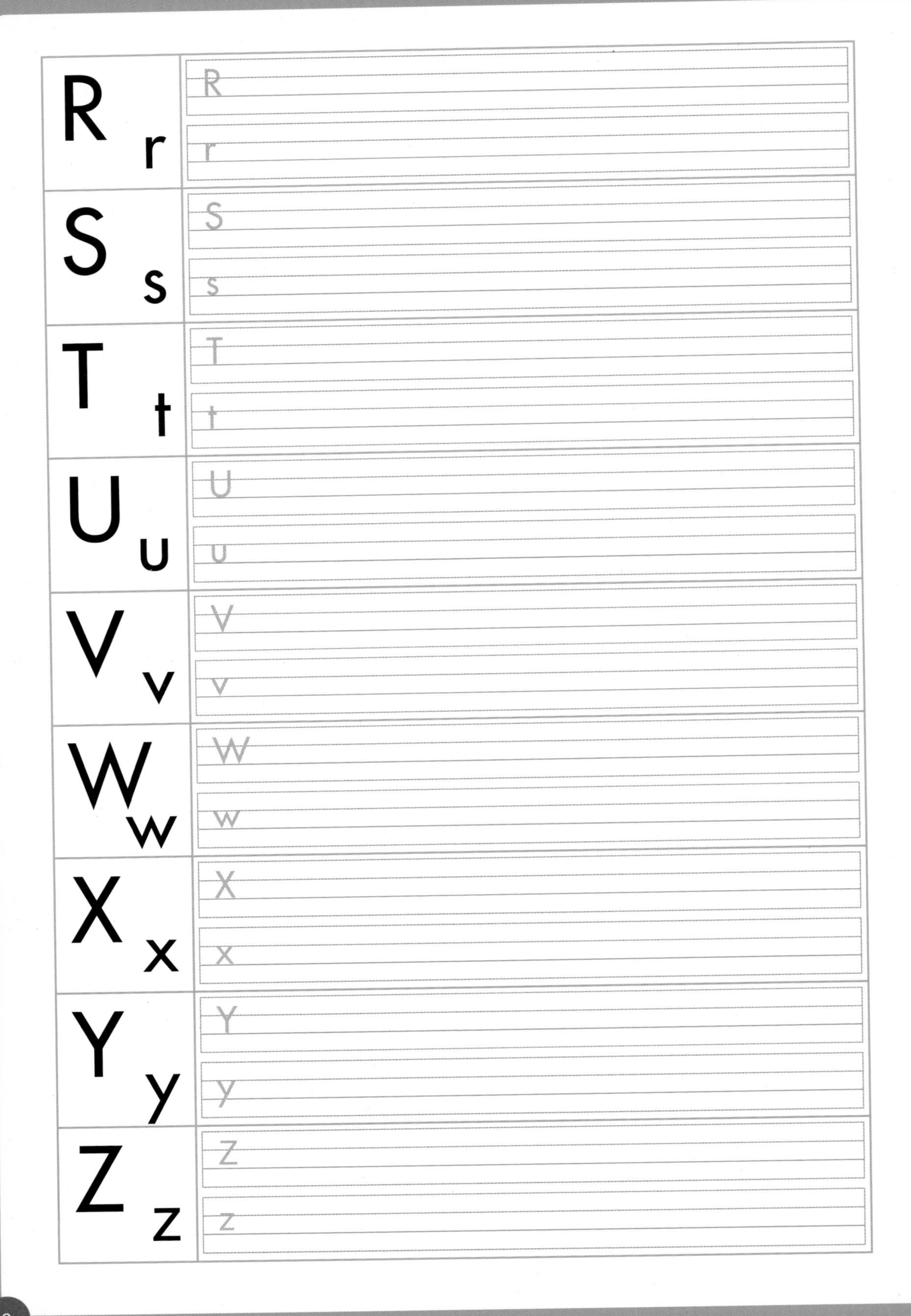

R r	R r
S s	S s
T t	T t
U u	U u
V v	V v
W w	W w
X x	X x
Y y	Y y
Z z	Z z

LESSON 1 (ONE)

I AM A BOY.

	I am a boy.
	I am a girl.
	I am a student.
	I am a teacher.
	I am a doctor.
	I am a nurse.

NEW WORDS

1
I
2
boy
3
girl
4
student
5
teacher
6
doctor
7
nurse
8
Tom
9
Jack
10
Jane
11
Mary
12
Jun-ho
13
Chan-ho
14
Mr. Brown
15
Mrs. Brown
16
Miss Brown

PATTERN PRACTICE

1. I am a boy. 2. I am Tom. 3. I am Jack.	10. I am a teacher. 11. I am Mr. Brown. 12. I am Mr. Kim.
4. I am a girl. 5. I am Jane. 6. I am Mary.	13. I am a doctor. 14. I am Mrs. Brown. 15. I am Mrs. Kim.
7. I am a student. 8. I am Jun-ho. 9. I am Chan-ho.	16. I am a nurse 17. I am Miss Brown. 18. I am Miss Kim.

1. 문장의 첫 글자는 대문자로 쓴다.
2. 문장이 끝나면 반드시 마침표(period)를 찍는다.
3. 사람의 이름은 문장 어디서든지 첫 글자를 대문자로 쓴다.
4. [Mr., Mrs., Miss, Ms.]의 첫 글자는 대문자로 쓴다.
5. 사람의 이름 앞에는 a를 붙이지 않는다.
6. 우리 말로 해석할 때 a의 뜻을 해석하지 않는다.

다음 그림을 보고 단어를 영어로 써 보세요.

1.	2.	3.	4.
5.	6.	7.	8.

다음 문장을 영어로 말해 보세요. (영어로 읽기 소요시간:)

1. 나는 소년입니다.

2. 나는 소녀입니다.

3. 나는 학생입니다.

4. 나는 선생님입니다.

6. 나는 의사입니다.

7. 나는 간호사입니다.

LESSON 2 (TWO)

YOU ARE A FARMER.

	You are a farmer.
	You are a driver.
	You are a cook.
	You are a policeman.
	You are a mailman.
	You are a pianist.

NEW WORDS

1
you
2
farmer
3
driver
4
cook
5
policeman
6
mailman
7
pianist
8
Korean
9
American
10
English
11
Canadian
12
Chinese
13
French
14
Mr. Smith
15
Mr. Wang
16
Miss Vincent

[You are ____________.]의 문형

1. You are a farmer. 2. You are Mr. Kim. 3. You are Korean.	10. You are a policeman. 11. You are Mr. Smith 12. You are Canadian.
4. You are a driver. 5. You are Mr. Brown. 6. You are American.	13. You are a mailman. 14. You are Mr. Wang. 15. You are Chinese.
7. You are a cook. 8. You are Mrs. Brown. 9. You are English.	16. You are a pianist. 17. You are Miss Vincent. 18. You are French.

1. 자기 자신의 이름이나 신분을 말할 때:
I am ········· . (나는 ·········입니다.)

2. 상대방의 이름이나 신분을 말할 때:
You are ·········. (당신은 ·········.입니다.)

3. 제 삼자의 이름이나 신분을 말할 때:
He is ········· . (그는 ·········. 입니다.)

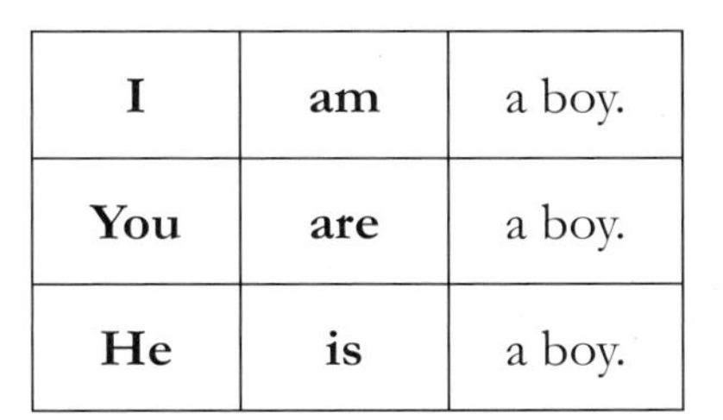

I	am	a boy.
You	are	a boy.
He	is	a boy.

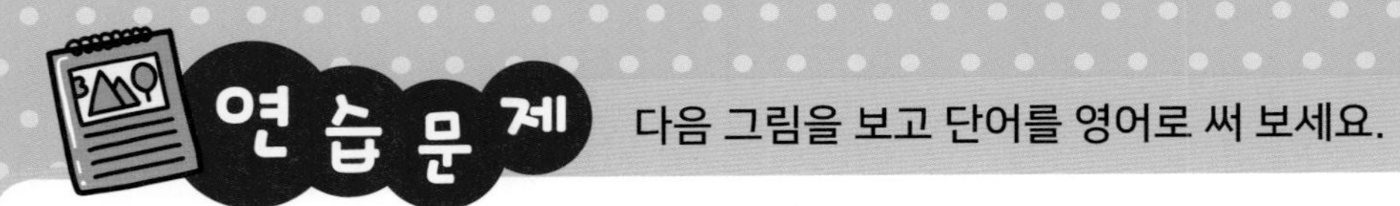

다음 그림을 보고 단어를 영어로 써 보세요.

1.	2.	3.	4.
5.	6.	7.	8.

다음 문장을 영어로 말해 보세요. (영어로 읽기 소요시간:)

1. 당신은 농부입니다.

2. 당신은 운전기사입니다.

3. 당신은 요리사입니다.

4. 당신은 경찰관입니다.

5. 당신은 우체부입니다.

6. 당신은 피아니스트입니다.

LESSON 3 (THREE)

HE IS MY FATHER.

	He is my father.
	She is your mother.
	Tom is his brother.
	Jane is her sister
	This is my uncle.
	That is your aunt.

NEW WORDS

1	2	3	4
he	she	father	mother
5	6	7	8
brother	sister	uncle	aunt
9	10	11	12
grandfather	grandmother	son	daughter
13	14	15	16
cousin	husband	wife	baby

[He is ____________.] 의 문형

1. He is my father. 2. He is my grandfather. 3. He is my uncle.	10. Jane is her sister. 11. Jane is her daughter. 12. Jane is her cousin.
4. She is your mother. 5. She is your grandmother. 6. She is your aunt.	13. My father is a farmer. 14. My mother is a cook. 15. My brother is a policeman.
7. Tom is his brother. 8. Tom is his son. 9. Tom is his cousin.	16. Your sister is a pianist. 17. Your son is a mailman. 18. Your daughter is a driver.

NOTE

I (나는)
my(나의)

I am a teacher.

My father is a teacher.

he(그는)
his(그의)

He is a doctor.

His mother is a doctor.

you(당신은)
your(당신의)

You are a student.

Your brother is a student.

she(그녀는)
her(그녀의)

She is a nurse.

Her sister is a nurse.

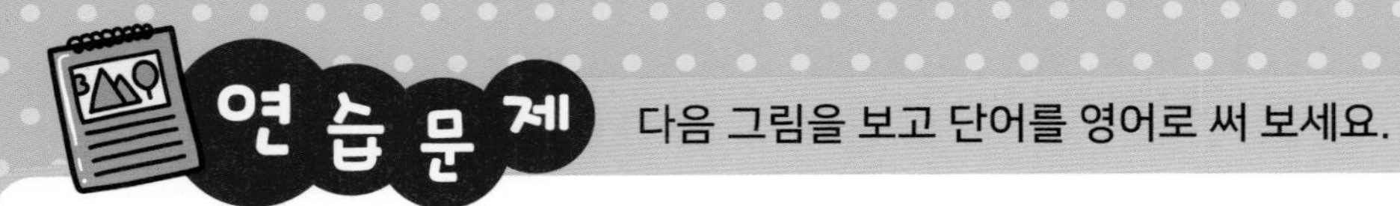

1.	2.	3.	4.
5.	6.	7.	8.

다음 문장을 영어로 말해 보세요. (영어로 읽기 소요시간:)

1. 그는 나의 아버지입니다.

2. 그녀는 당신의 어머니입니다.

3. 탐은 그의 형제입니다.

4. 제인은 그녀의 자매입니다.

5. 이 분은 나의 아저씨입니다.

6. 저 분은 당신의 아주머니입니다.

LESSON 4 (FOUR)

THIS IS A BOOK.

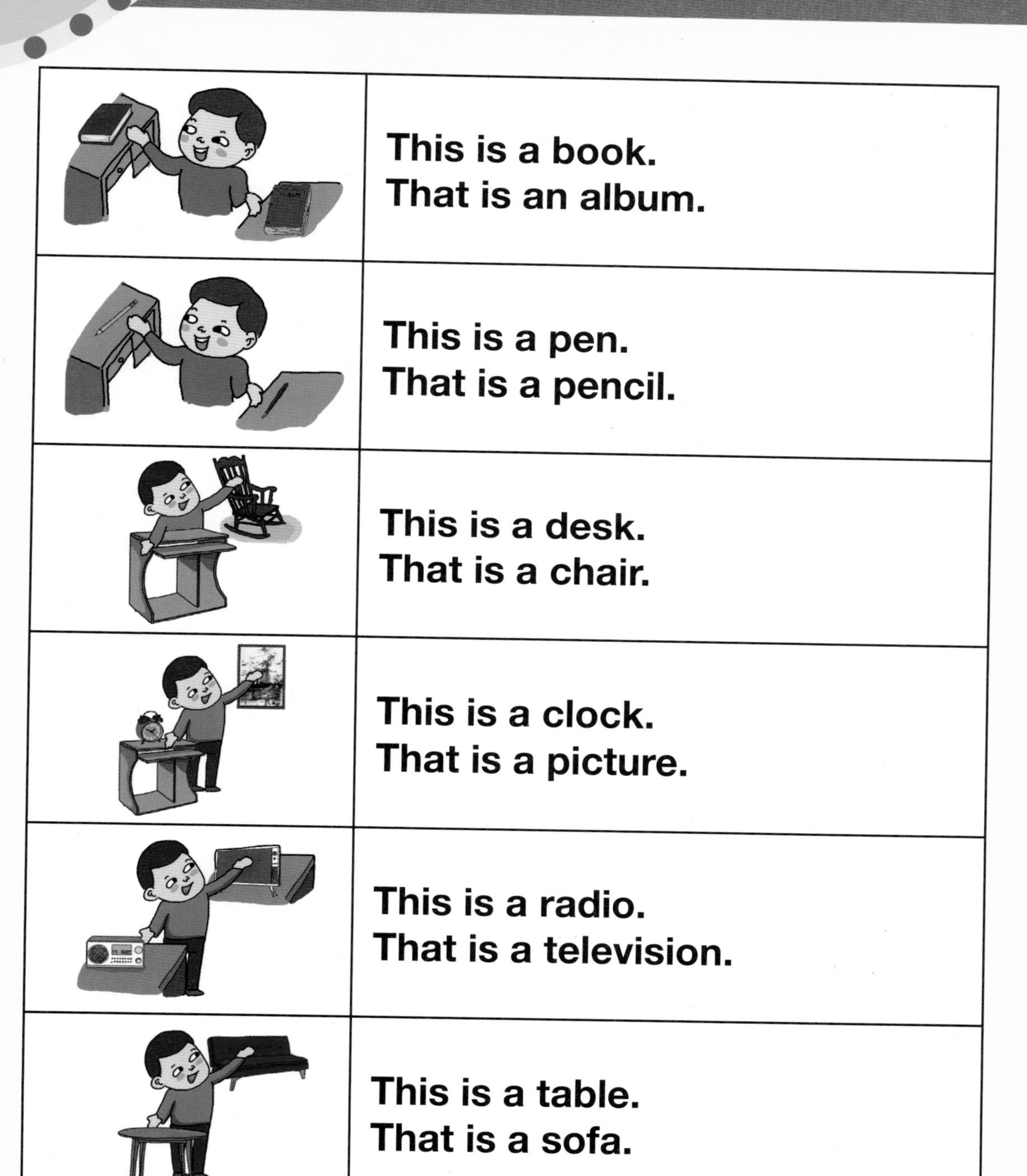

	This is a book. That is an album.
	This is a pen. That is a pencil.
	This is a desk. That is a chair.
	This is a clock. That is a picture.
	This is a radio. That is a television.
	This is a table. That is a sofa.

NEW WORDS

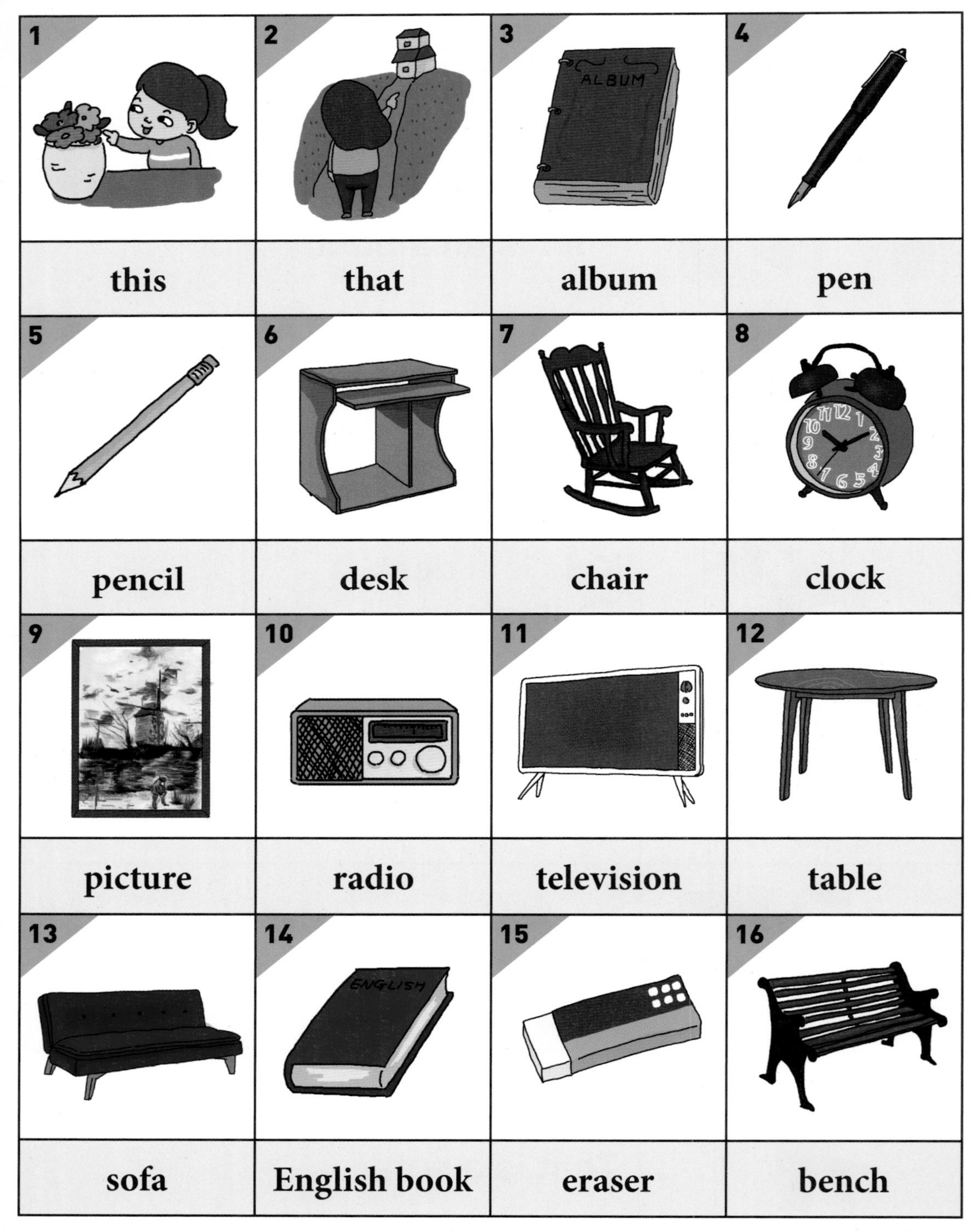
1
this
2
that
3
ALBUM
album
4
pen
5
pencil
6
desk
7
chair
8
clock
9
picture
10
radio
11
television
12
table
13
sofa
14
ENGLISH
English book
15
eraser
16
bench

[This is ____________.] 의 문형

1. This is a book. 2. This is an album. 3. This is an English book.	10. That is a clock. 11. That is a picture. 12. That is my father.
4. This is a pen. 5. This is a pencil. 6. This is an eraser.	13. That is a radio. 14. That is a television. 15. That is your mother.
7. This is a desk. 8. This is a chair. 9. This is a bench.	16. That is a table. 17. That is a sofa. 18. That is his brother.

다음 그림을 보고 단어를 영어로 써 보세요.

1.	2.	3.	4.
5.	6.	7.	8.

다음 문장을 영어로 말해 보세요. (영어로 읽기 소요시간:)

1. 이것은 책입니다.
   저것은 앨범입니다.

2. 이것은 펜입니다.
   저것은 연필입니다.

3. 이것은 책상입니다.
   저것은 의자입니다.

4. 이것은 시계입니다.
   저것은 그림입니다.

5. 이것은 라디오입니다.
   저것은 텔레비전입니다.

6. 이것은 탁자입니다.
   저것은 소파입니다.

LESSON 5 (FIVE)

WE ARE BOYS.

	I am a boy. We are boys.
	You are a girl. You are girls.
	He is a student. They are students.
	This is my book. These are our books.
	That is your pencil. Those are your pencils.
	It is his eraser. They are their erasers.

NEW WORDS

1
we
2
you
3
they
4
these
5
those
6
boys
7
girls
8
students
9
books
10
pencils
11
erasers
12
doctors
13
nurses
14
Koreans
15
Americans
16
Chinese

PATTERN PRACTICE

[We are ______________.] 의 문형

1. I am a doctor. 2. We are doctors.	9. This is an Englishman. 10. These are Englishmen.
3. You are a nurse. 4. You are nurses.	11. That is a Chinese. 12. Those are Chinese.
5. He is a Korean. 6. They are Koreans.	13. It is his album. 14. They are their albums.
7. She is an American. 8. They are Americans.	15. This is my English book. 16. These are our English books.

NOTE

* 1개를 단수라고 하고, 2개 이상을 복수라고 한다.

단수	복수	단수	복수	단수	복수
I	we	my	our	a student	students
you	you	your	your	a book	books
he	they	his	their	a pencil	pencils
she	they	her	their	an eraser	erasers
this	these	its	their	a Korean	Koreans
that	those	a boy	boys	an American	Americans
it	they	a girl	girls	a Chinese	Chinese

다음 그림을 보고 단어를 영어로 써 보세요.

1.	2.	3.	4.
5.	6.	7.	8.

다음 문장을 영어로 말해 보세요. (영어로 읽기 소요시간:)

1. 나는 소년입니다.
   우리는 소년들입니다.

2. 당신은 소녀입니다.
   당신들은 소녀들입니다.

3. 그는 학생입니다.
   그들은 학생들입니다.

4. 이것은 나의 책입니다.
   이것들은 우리의 책들입니다.

5. 저것은 당신의 연필입니다.
   저것들은 당신들의 연필들입니다.

6. 그것은 그의 지우개입니다.
   그것들은 그들의 지우개들입니다.

LESSON 6(SIX)

I AM NOT TOM.

I am John.
I am not Tom.

You are a fireman.
You are not a policeman.

He is American.
He is not English.

This is an apple.
This is not an orange.

That is a banana.
That is not a strawberry.

It is a lemon.
It is not a melon.

NEW WORDS

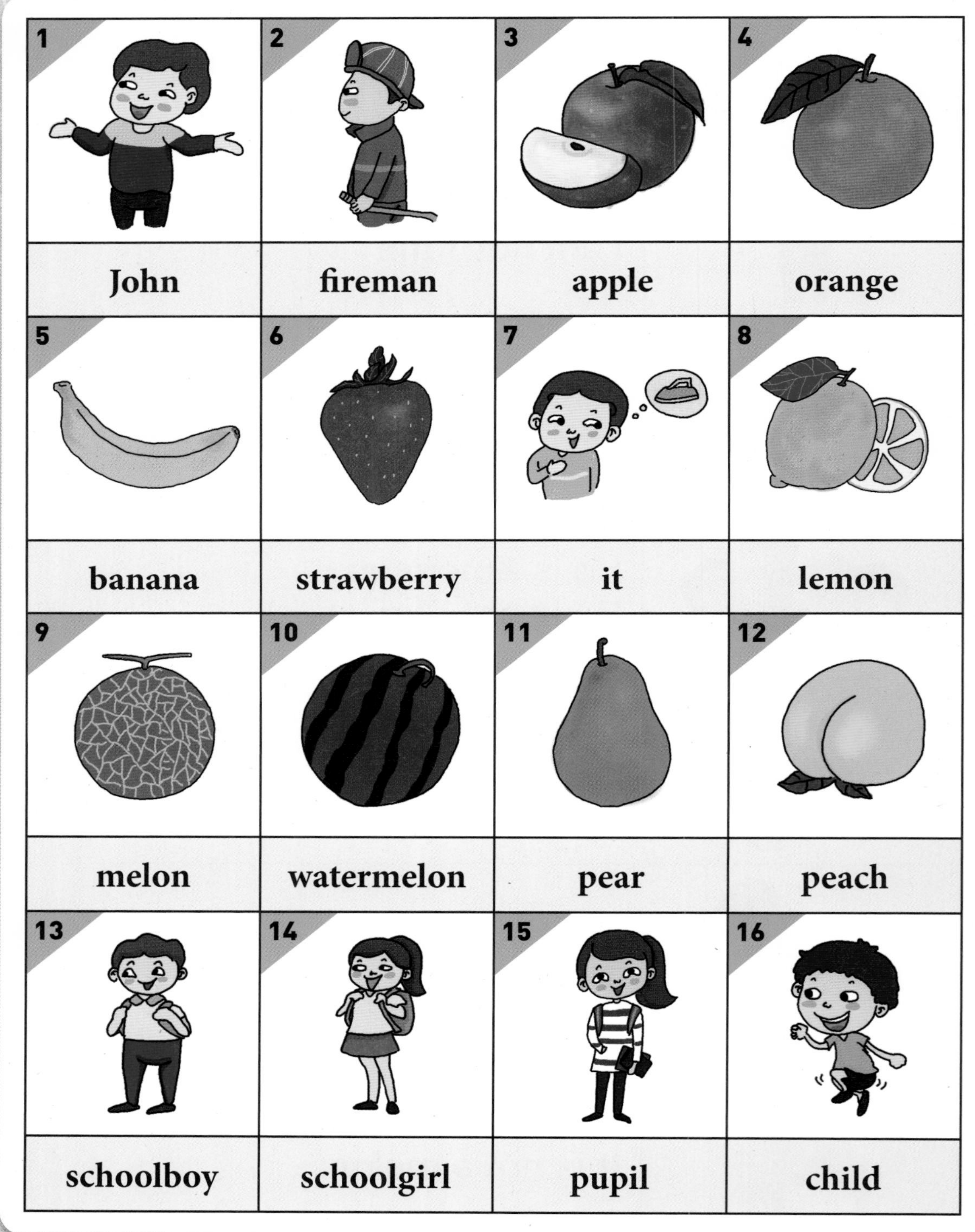
1
John
2
fireman
3
apple
4
orange
5
banana
6
strawberry
7
it
8
lemon
9
melon
10
watermelon
11
pear
12
peach
13
schoolboy
14
schoolgirl
15
pupil
16
child

PATTERN PRACTICE

[I am not ______________.]의 문형

1. I am not John. 2. I am not a pupil. 3. I am not a schoolboy.	10. This is not an apple. 11. This is not an orange. 12. This is not a watermelon.
4. You are not Mary. 5. You are not a pupil. 6. You are not a schoolgirl.	13. That is not a banana. 14. That is not a strawberry. 15. That is not a pear.
7. He is not American. 8. He is not English. 9. He is not a child.	16. It is not a lemon. 17. It is not a melon. 18. It is not a peach.

NOTE

* 문장의 종류

(1) 긍정문: [··················입니다.]
(2) 부정문: [············이 아닙니다.]
(3) 의문문: [··················입니까?]

예 I am a student.
I am not a student.
Am I a student?

* a와 an의 용법

a: 단어의 첫 소리가 자음일 때
an: 단어의 첫 소리가 모음일 때
모음: a, e, i, o, u
자음: b, c, d, f, g, ·········

예 a book, a dog, a student
a desk, a pen, a teacher
an apple, an orange

LESSON 6

다음 그림을 보고 단어를 영어로 써 보세요.

1.	2.	3.	4.
5.	6.	7.	8.

다음 문장을 영어로 말해 보세요. (영어로 읽기 소요시간:)

1. 나는 존입니다.
   나는 탐이 아닙니다.

2. 당신은 소방관입니다.
   당신은 경찰관이 아닙니다.

3. 그는 미국인입니다.
   그는 영국인이 아닙니다.

4. 이것은 사과입니다.
   이것은 오렌지가 아닙니다.

5. 저것은 바나나입니다.
   저것은 딸기가 아닙니다.

6. 그것은 레몬입니다.
   그것은 멜론이 아닙니다.

LESSON 7 (SEVEN)

ARE YOU A SINGER?

	**Are you a singer?** **Yes, I am.**
	**Are you a pilot?** **No, I am not. I'm a driver.**
	**Am I a cowboy?** **Yes, you are.**
	**Am I a fisherman?** **No, you aren't. You're a farmer.**
	**Is he a scientist?** **Yes, he is.**
	**Is she Miss Brown?** **No, she isn't. She is Mrs. Brown.**

NEW WORDS

1	2	3	4
one	two	three	four

5	6	7	8
five	six	seven	singer

9	10	11	12
yes	pilot	no	cowboy

13	14	15	16
fisherman	scientist	baker	artist

PATTERN PRACTICE

[Are you ______________ ?] 의 문형

1. Are you a baker? 2. Yes, I am. 3. Yes, I'm a baker.	10. Is the girl American? 11. No, she isn't. 12. No, she isn't American.
4. Are you an artist? 5. No, I'm not. 6. No, I'm not an artist.	13. Is the boy English? 14. No, he's not. 15. No, he's not English.
7. Is he a pupil? 8. Yes, he is. 9. Yes, he's a pupil.	16. Is Miss Brown a cook? 17. Yes, she is. 18. Yes, she's a cook.

NOTE

* 질문에 대한 대답하는 방법

질문 ································ 대답

(1) you ································ I

(2) I ································ you

(3) he ································ he

(4) she ································ she

(5) this ································ it

(6) that ································ it

(7) it ································ it

(8) Tom ································ he

(9) Jane ································ she

예 Are you a student?
Yes, I am.
Are you a student?
No, I'm not.
Am I a student?
Yes, you are.
Am I a student?
No, you're not.
Am I a student?
No, you aren't a student.
Is he a student?
Yes, he is.
Is Tom a student?
No, he's not.

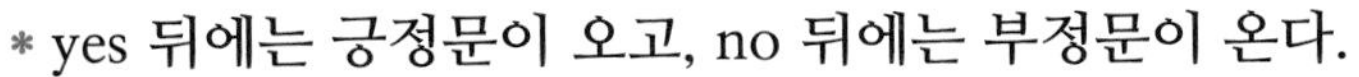

* yes 뒤에는 긍정문이 오고, no 뒤에는 부정문이 온다.

다음 그림을 보고 단어를 영어로 써 보세요.

1.	2.	3.	4.
5.	6.	7.	8.

다음 문장을 영어로 말해 보세요. (영어로 읽기 소요시간:)

1. 당신은 가수입니까?
예, 그렇습니다.

2. 당신은 비행기 조종사입니까?
아니오, 그렇지 않습니다.
나는 운전기사입니다.

3. 내가 목동입니까?
예, 그렇습니다.

4. 내가 어부입니까?
아니오, 그렇지 않습니다.
당신은 농부입니다.

5. 그는 과학자입니까?
예, 그렇습니다.

6. 그녀는 브라운양입니까?
아니오, 그렇지 않습니다.
그녀는 브라운 여사입니다.

LESSON 8 (EIGHT)

IS THIS A MAP?

	Is this a map? Yes, it is.
	Is this a tiger? No, it isn't. It's a lion.
	Is that an elephant? Yes, it is.
	Is that a fox? No, it isn't. It's a wolf.
	Is that a window? No, it isn't.
	What is it, then? It's a door.

NEW WORDS

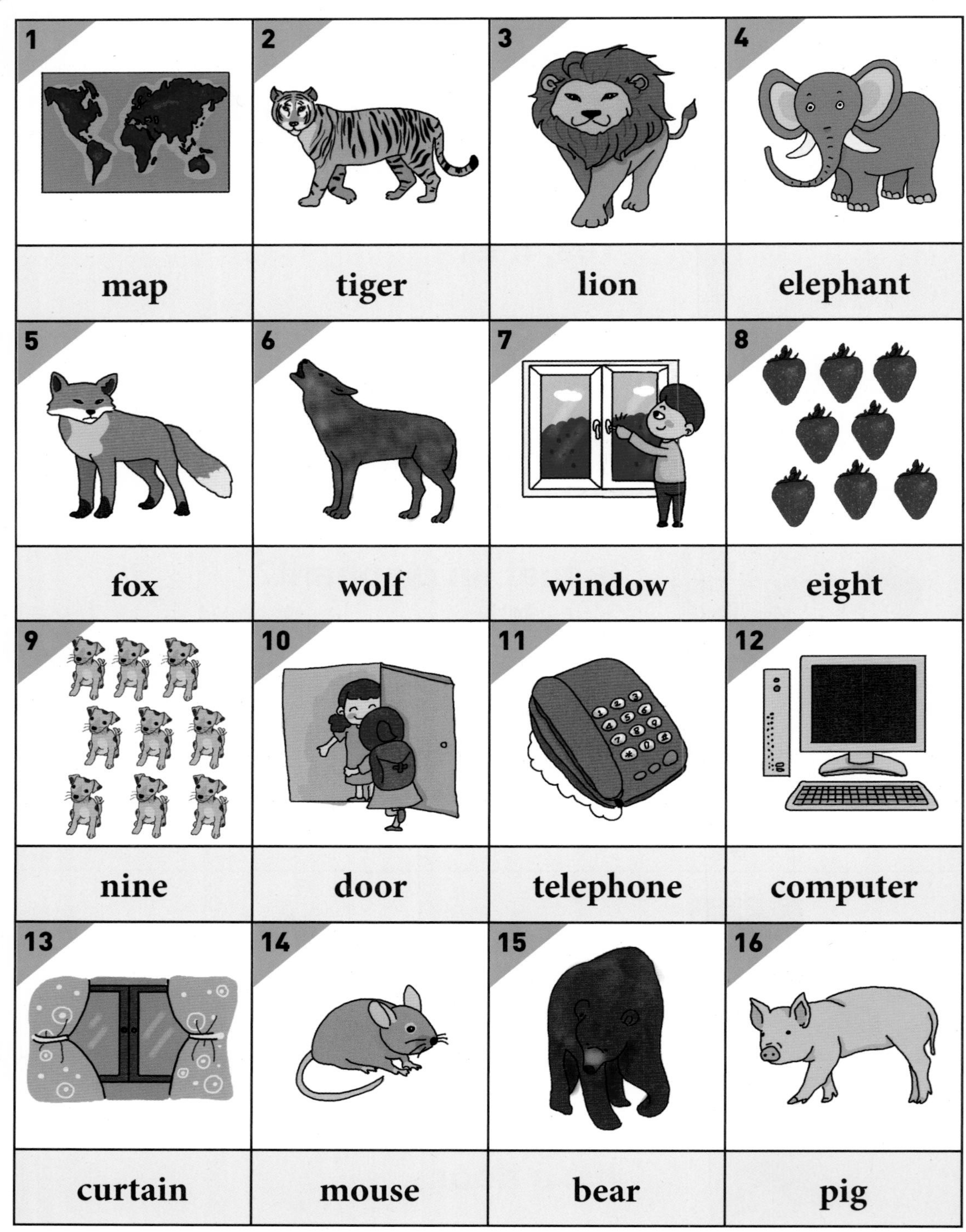
1
map
2
tiger
3
lion
4
elephant
5
fox
6
wolf
7
window
8
eight
9
nine
10
door
11
telephone
12
computer
13
curtain
14
mouse
15
bear
16
pig

[Is this ____________?] 의 문형

1. Is this a telephone? 2. Yes, it is. 3. Yes, it is a telephone.	10. Is that a mouse? 11. No, it isn't. 12. No, it isn't a mouse.
4. Are these calendars? 5. No, they aren't. 6. No, they're not calendars.	13. Is this a bear? 14. Yes, it is. 15. Yes, it is a bear.
7. Are those curtains? 8. Yes, they are. 9. Yes, they're curtains.	16. Is that a pig? 17. No, it isn't. 18. No, it isn't a pig.

NOTE

* 주어와 be동사의 줄인 말

(1) I am = I'm

(2) you are = you're

(3) he is = he's

(4) she is = she's

(5) that is = that's

(6) it is = it's

* be동사와 not의 줄인 말

(1) are not = aren't

(2) is not = isn't

* this, that, it의 용법

this: 가까운 것

that: 먼 곳의 것

it: 보이지 않는 것을 가리킬 때

다음 그림을 보고 단어를 영어로 써 보세요.

1.	2.	3.	4.
5.	6.	7.	8.

다음 문장을 영어로 말해 보세요. (영어로 읽기 소요시간:)

1. 이것은 지도입니까?
   예, 그렇습니다.

2. 이것은 호랑이입니까?
   아니오, 그렇지 않습니다.
   그것은 사자입니다.

3. 저것은 코끼리입니까?
   예,그렇습니다.

4. 저것은 여우입니까?
   아니오, 그렇지 않습니다.
   그것은 늑대입니다.

5. 저것은 창문입니까?
   아니오, 그렇지 않습니다.

6. 그러면, 그것은 무엇입니까?
   그것은 문입니다.

LESSON 9 (NINE)

WHAT IS THIS?

	What is this? It is a blackboard.
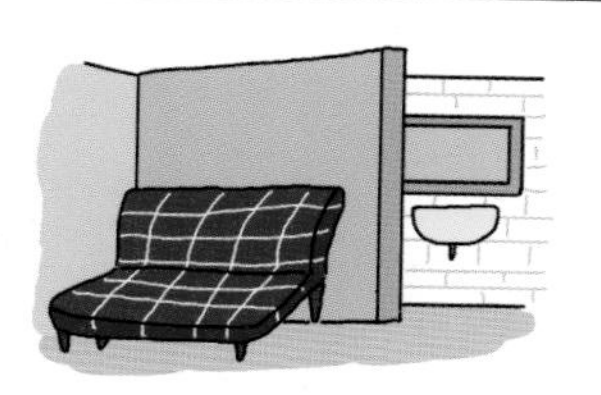	What is that? It is a wall.
	What is this? It is a dog.
	What is that? It is a cat.
	What is your name? My name is Han-na.
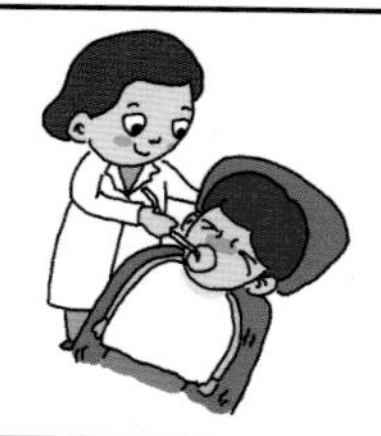	What is she? She is a dentist.

NEW WORDS

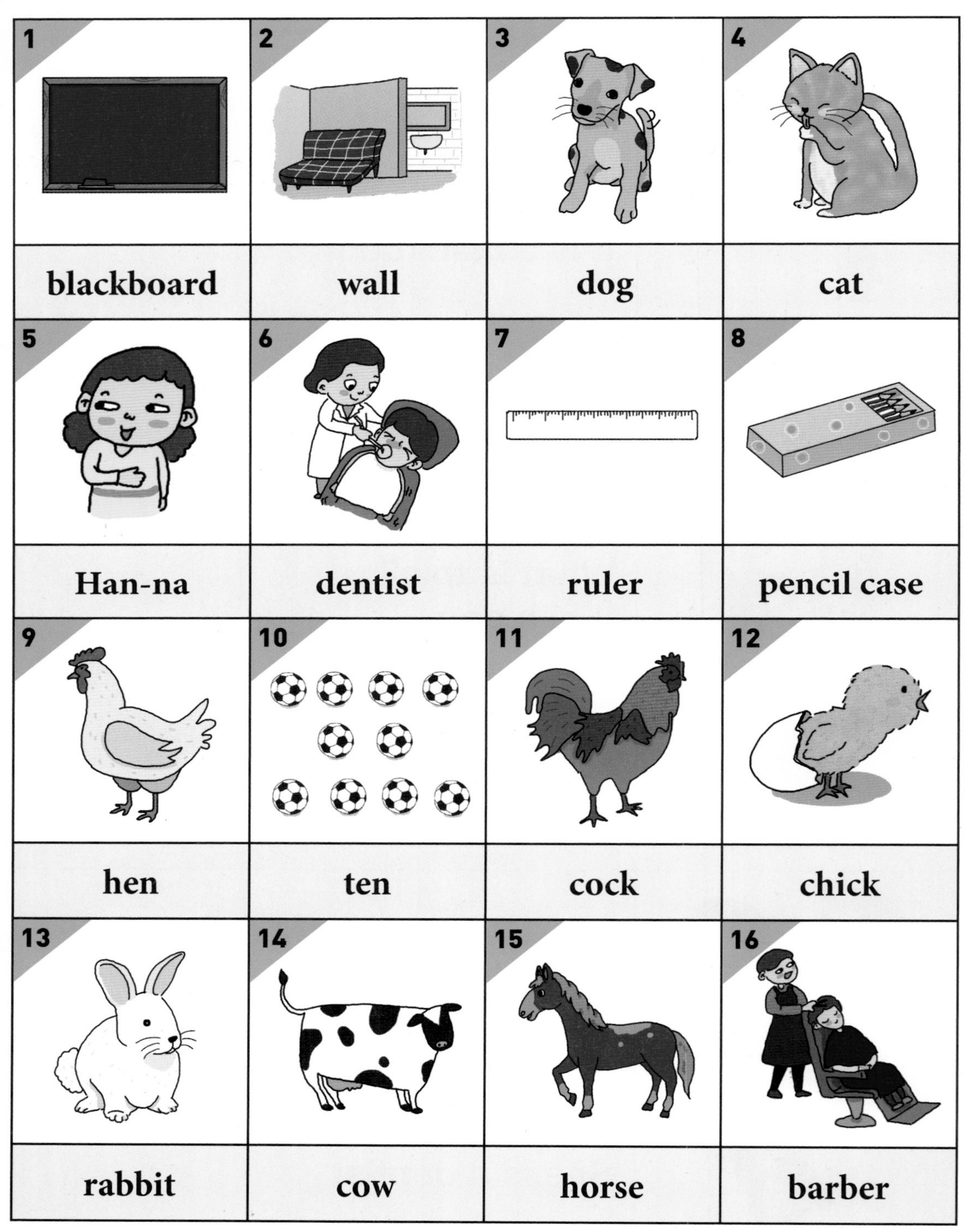
1 blackboard
2 wall
3 dog
4 cat
5 Han-na
6 dentist
7 ruler
8 pencil case
9 hen
10 ten
11 cock
12 chick
13 rabbit
14 cow
15 horse
16 barber

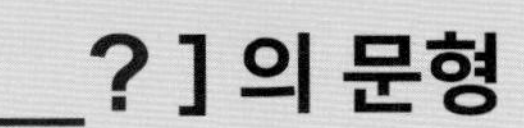

[What is ____________?] 의 문형

1. What is this? 2. It is a knife.	9. What are these? 10. They are chicks.
3. What is that? 4. It is a pencil case.	11. What are those? 12. They are rabbits.
5. What is this? 6. It is a hen.	13. What are these? 14. They are cows.
7. What is that? 8. It is a cock.	15. What are those? 16. They are horses.

NOTE

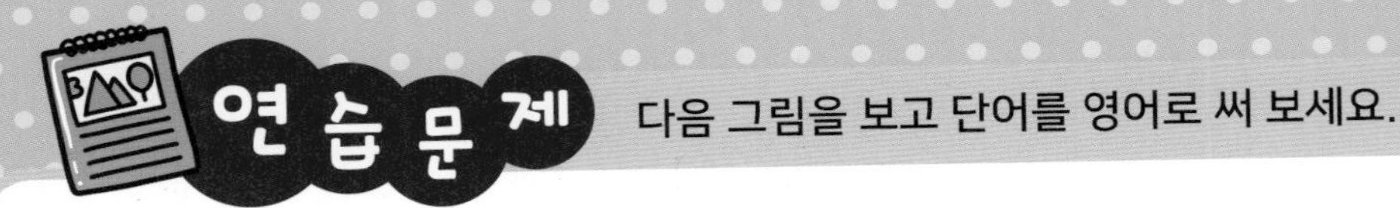

연습문제 다음 그림을 보고 단어를 영어로 써 보세요.

1.	2.	3.	4.
5.	6.	7.	8.

다음 문장을 영어로 말해 보세요. (영어로 읽기 소요시간:)

1. 이것은 무엇입니까?
   그것은 칠판입니다.

2. 저것은 무엇입니까?
   그것은 벽입니다.

3. 이것은 무엇입니까?
   그것은 개입니다.

4. 저것은 무엇입니까?
   그것은 고양이입니다.

5. 당신의 이름은 무엇입니까?
   나의 이름은 한나입니다.

6. 그녀는 무얼 하시는 분입니까?
   그녀는 치과 의사입니다.

LESSON 10 (TEN)

WHO ARE YOU?

	Who are you? I am John.
	Who are you? I am his brother.
	Who is he? He is Mr. Brown.
	Who is he? He is my father.
	What is your father? He is a policeman.
	What is your sister? My sister is a nurse.

NEW WORDS

1	2	3	4
11	12	13	14
eleven	twelve	thirteen	fourteen
5	6	7	8
15	16	17	18
fifteen	sixteen	seventeen	eighteen
9	10	11	12
19	20	21	
nineteen	twenty	twenty one	Jane
13	14	15	16
lady	gentleman	man	woman

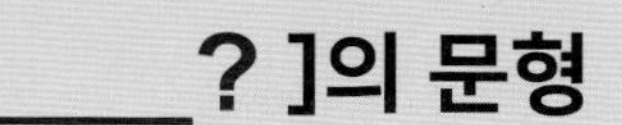

[Who are ＿＿＿＿＿＿＿＿?]의 문형

1. Who are you? 2. I am Jane.	9. Who is the lady? 10. She is Miss Kim.
3. Who are you? 4. I am her sister.	11. Who is the gentleman? 12. He is my father.
5. Who am I? 6. You are Chan-ho.	13. Who is this man? 14. He is Mr. Kim.
7. Who am I? 8. You are his brother.	15. What is this woman? 16. She is a doctor.

* 의문문의 종류

(1) 의문사가 없는 의문문: yes 나 no로 대답하고, 꼬리를 올려 읽는다.

(2) 의문사가 있는 의문문: yes 나 no로 대답하지 않고, 꼬리를 내려 읽는다.

예 Is this a book? (↗)
Yes, it is.

Is this a book?(↗)
No, it isn't.

What is this?(↘)
It is a book.

다음 그림을 보고 단어를 영어로 써 보세요.

11	12	13	20
1.	2.	3.	4.
5.	6.	7.	8.

다음 문장을 영어로 말해 보세요. (영어로 읽기 소요시간:)

1. 당신은 누구입니까?
   나는 존입니다.

2. 당신은 누구입니까?
   나는 그의 형제입니다.

3. 그는 누구입니까?
   그는 브라운씨입니다.

4. 그는 누구입니까?
   그는 나의 아버지입니다.

5. 당신의 아버지는 무엇 하시는 분입니까?
   그는 경찰관입니다.

6. 당신의 누님은 무엇 하시는 분입니까?
   나의 누님은 간호사입니다.

LESSON 11 (ELEVEN)

WHERE IS YOUR HOUSE?

	Where is your house? It is in Seoul.
	Where is the cat? It is under the table.
	Where is my lunch box? It is on the desk.
	Where is your brother? He is by the window.
	Where is your mother? My mother is in the kitchen.
	Where is your father? He is in the living room.

NEW WORDS

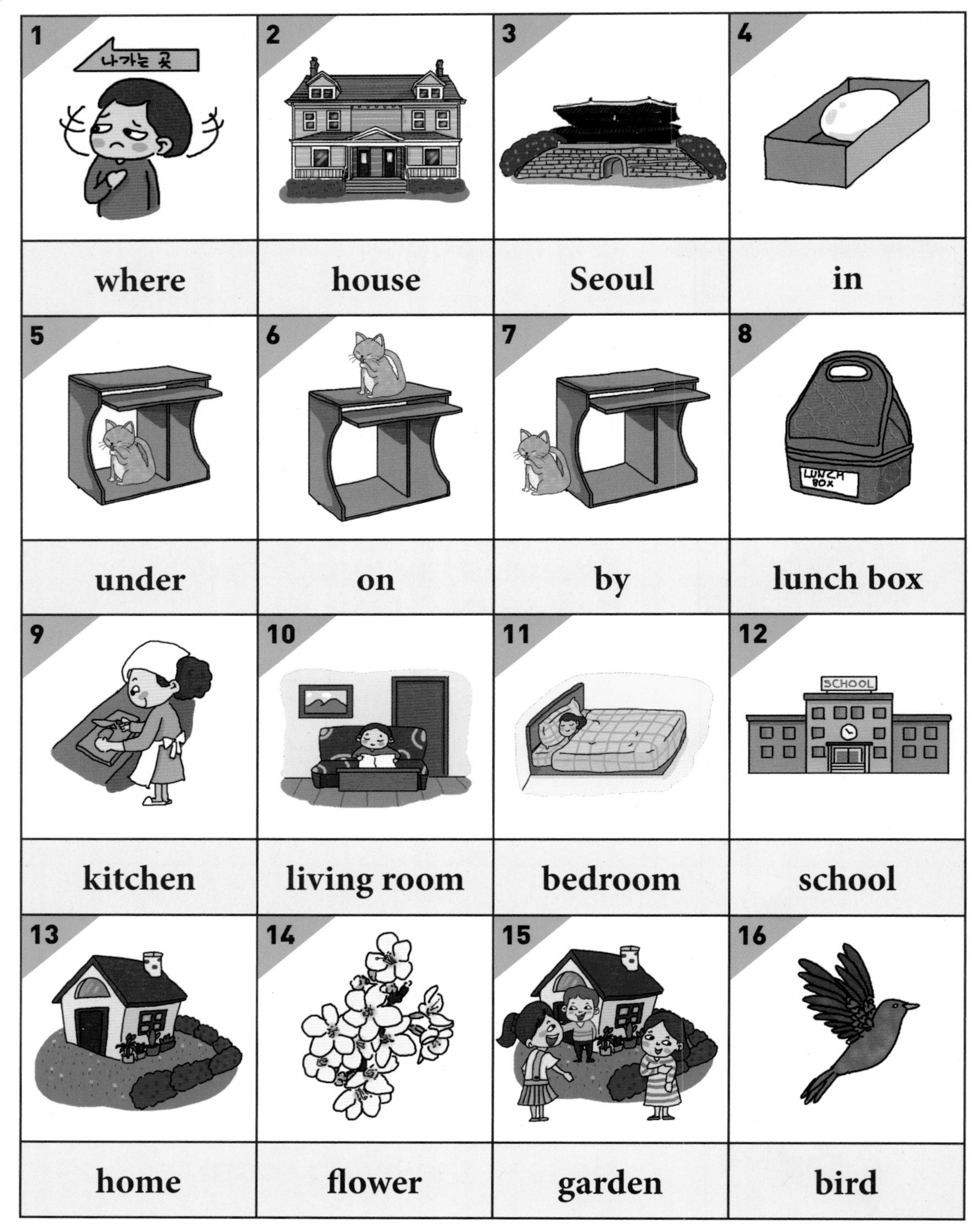
1
나가는 곳
where
2
house
3
Seoul
4
in
5
under
6
on
7
by
8
LUNCH BOX
lunch box
9
kitchen
10
living room
11
bedroom
12
SCHOOL
school
13
home
14
flower
15
garden
16
bird

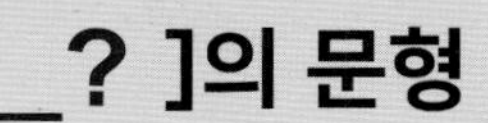

[Where is ____________?]의 문형

1. Where is your mother? 2. She is in the bedroom.	9. Where are the birds? 10. They are in the garden.
3. Where is your friend? 4. He is at school.	11. Where is your mother's pen? 12. It is on the table.
5. Where is your sister? 6. She is at home.	13. Where is your baby? 14. My baby is in the living room.
7. Where are the flowers? 8. They are in the garden.	15. Where is the map? 16. It is on the wall.

* 의문사의 종류

(1) what(무엇): 사물이나 사람의 직업을 물을 때

(2) who(누구): 사람의 이름이나 가족관계를 물을 때

(3) where(어디): 장소를 물을 때

(4) when(때): 시간을 물을 때

(5) why(왜): 이유를 물을 때

(6) how(어떻게): 방법을 물을 때

* 의문사는 의문문에서 항상 문장 앞에 놓는다.

다음 그림을 보고 단어를 영어로 써 보세요.

1.	**2.**	**3.**	**4.**
5.	**6.**	**7.**	**8.**

다음 문장을 영어로 말해 보세요. (영어로 읽기 소요시간:)

1. 당신의 집은 어디에 있습니까?
나의 집은 서울에 있습니다.

2. 그 고양이는 어디에 있습니까?
그것은 탁자 아래에 있습니다.

3. 나의 도시락은 어디에 있습니까?
그것은 책상 위에 있습니다.

4. 당신의 남동생은 어디에 있습니까?
그는 창문 옆에 있습니다.

5. 당신의 어머니는 어디에 계십니까?
나의 어머니는 부엌에 계십니다.

6. 당신의 아버지는 어디에 계십니까?
그는 거실에 있습니다.

LESSON 12 (TWELVE)

I AM TALL.

	I am tall. You are short.
	He is old. She is young.
	Tom is handsome. Jane is pretty.
 	Jun-ho is strong. Chan-ho is weak.
	Mrs. Brown is fat. Miss Brown is thin.
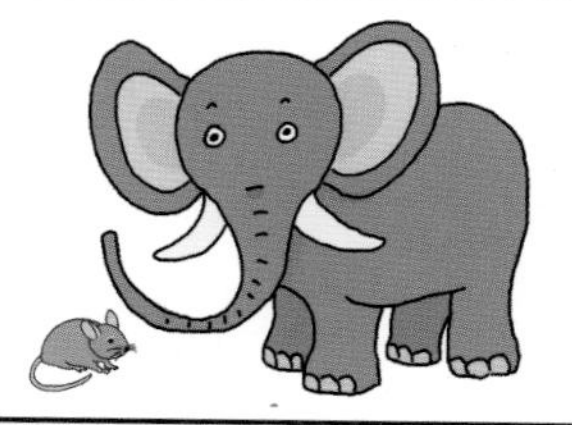	The elephant is heavy. The mouse is light.

NEW WORDS

1
tall
2
short
3
old
4
young
5
handsome
6
pretty
7
strong
8
weak
9
fat
10
thin
11
heavy
12
light
13
good
14
bad
15
kind
16
happy

[I am ____________.]의 문형

1. I am tall. 2. I am a boy. 3. I am a tall boy.	10. She is kind. 11. She is a girl. 12. She is a kind girl.
4. You are good. 5. You are a teacher. 6. You are a good teacher.	13. Min-hee is happy. 14. Min-hee is a lady. 15. Min-hee is a happy lady.
7. He is bad. 8. He is a man. 9. He is a bad man.	16. We are busy. 17. We are students. 18. We are busy students.

* 형용사의 2가지 용법

(1) be동사와 같이 쓰여서 마치 동사처럼 쓰인다.
(2) 명사 앞에 놓여서 명사를 수식한다.

예 Jane is pretty. (제인은 예쁘다.)
Jane is a pretty girl. (제인은 예쁜 소녀이다.)

* this의 2가지 용법

(1) this가 홀로 쓰이면 this의 뜻은 [이것]으로 해석한다.
(2) this가 명사 앞에 놓여 쓰이면 this의 뜻은 [이]로 해석한다.

예 This is my book. (이것은 나의 책이다.)
This book is mine. (이 책은 나의 것이다.)

다음 그림을 보고 단어를 영어로 써 보세요.

1.	2.	3.	4.
5.	6.	7.	8.

다음 문장을 영어로 말해 보세요. (영어로 읽기 소요시간:)

1. 나는 키가 크다.
   당신은 키가 작다.
2. 그는 나이가 많다.
   그녀는 나이가 어리다.
3. 탐은 미남이다.
   제인은 예쁘다.
4. 준호는 힘이 세다.
   찬호는 약하다.
5. 브라운 여사는 뚱뚱하다.
   브라운 양은 날씬하다.
6. 코끼리는 무겁다.
   쥐는 가볍다.

LESSON 13 (THIRTEEN)

THIS HOUSE IS BEAUTIFUL.

	This house is beautiful. That house is old.
	This car is big. That car is small.
	This pencil is long. That pencil is short.
	This shirt is clean. That shirt is dirty.
	This mountain is low. That mountain is high.
	This river is wide. That river is narrow.

NEW WORDS

1	2	3	4
beautiful	old	car	big
5	6	7	8
small	long	shirt	clean
9	10	11	12
dirty	mountain	high	low
13	14	15	16
river	wide	narrow	busy

1. This is a house. 2. This house is beautiful. 3. This is a beautiful house.	10. That is a shirt. 11. That shirt is clean. 12. That is a clean shirt.
4. This is a car. 5. This car is small. 6. This is a small car.	13. That is a mountain. 14. That mountain is high. 15. That is a high mountain.
7. This is a pencil. 8. This pencil is long. 9. This is a long pencil.	16. That is a river. 17. That river is narrow. 18. That is a narrow river.

다음 그림을 보고 단어를 영어로 써 보세요.

1.	2.	3.	4.
5.	6.	7.	8.

다음 문장을 영어로 말해 보세요. (영어로 읽기 소요시간:)

1. 이 집은 아름답다.
   저 집은 낡았다.

2. 이 자동차는 크다.
   저 자동차는 작다.

3. 이 연필은 길다.
   저 연필은 짧다.

4. 이 셔츠는 깨끗하다.
   저 셔츠는 더럽다.

5. 이 산은 낮다.
   저 산은 높다.

6. 이 강은 넓다.
   저 강은 좁다.

LESSON 14 (FOURTEEN)

IT IS HOT TODAY.

	It is hot today. It is hot in summer.
	It is cold this morning. It is cold in winter.
	It is warm this afternoon. It is warm in spring.
	It is cool this evening. It is cool in autumn.
	It is fine today. It is cloudy today.
	It is Sunday today. It is September 16th today.

NEW WORDS

1
hot
2
오늘
today
3
summer
4
cold
5
winter
6
warm
7
spring
8
cool
9
autumn
10
fine
11
cloudy
12
SUNDAY
Sunday
13
9月
September
14
3 MAR
this morning
15
7 JUL
this summer
16
12 DEC
this winter

[It is ______________.] 의 문형

1. It is hot today. 2. Today is hot. 3. It is hot this summer.	10. It is cool in the evening. 11. It is cool in autumn. 12. It is cool this autumn.
4. It is cold in the morning. 5. It is cold in winter. 6. It is cold this winter.	13. It is fine today. 14. It is cloudy today. 15. Today is cloudy.
7. It is warm in the afternoon. 8. It is warm in spring. 9. It is warm this spring.	16. It is Sunday today. 17. Today is Sunday. 18. Today is September 16th.

NOTE

* it의 특별 용법:

날씨, 요일, 날짜, 시간, 계절 등을 나타낼 때 it은 해석하지 않는다.

예 It is hot today. (오늘은 덥다.)

It is Sunday today. (오늘은 일요일이다.)

It is September 16th today. (오늘은 9월 16일이다.)

It is seven o'clock now. (지금은 7시이다.)

It is summer now. (지금은 여름이다.)

다음 그림을 보고 단어를 영어로 써 보세요.

다음 문장을 영어로 말해 보세요. (영어로 읽기 소요시간:)

1. 오늘은 덥다.
   여름에는 덥다.

2. 오늘 아침은 춥다.
   겨울에는 춥다.

3. 오늘 오후는 따스하다.
   봄에는 따스하다.

4. 오늘 저녁은 선선하다.
   가을에는 선선하다.

5. 오늘은 날씨가 좋다.
   오늘은 흐리다.

6. 오늘은 일요일이다.
   오늘은 9월 16일이다.

LESSON 15 (FIFTEEN)

I HAVE A BOOK.

	I have a book. I have many books.
	You have water. You have much water.
	He has a storybook. He has a lot of storybooks.
	She has a friend. She has two friends.
	John has breakfast at seven in the morning. Mary has lunch at twelve.
	I have dinner at seven in the evening. He has dinner at eight in the evening.

NEW WORDS

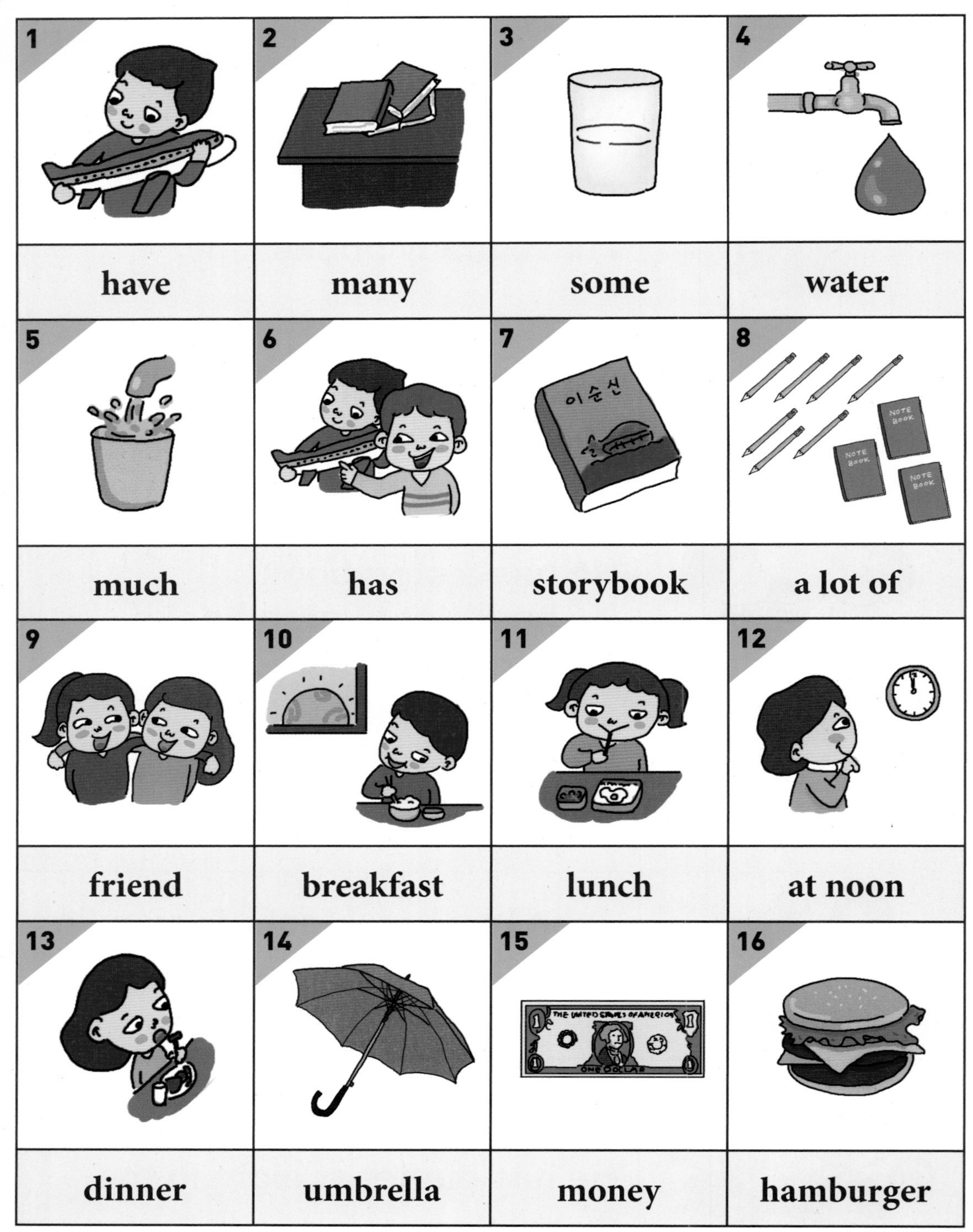
1 have
2 many
3 some
4 water
5 much
6 has
7 storybook
8 a lot of
9 friend
10 breakfast
11 lunch
12 at noon
13 dinner
14 umbrella
15 money
16 hamburger

PATTERN PRACTICE

[I have ________.]의 문항

1. I have an English book. 2. I have many English books. 3. I have a lot of English books.	10. She has some friends. 11. She has many friends. 12. She has a lot of friends.
4. You have an umbrella. 5. You have many umbrellas. 6. You have a lot of umbrellas.	13. Tom has some water. 14. Tom has much water. 15. Tom has a lot of water.
7. He has some money. 8. He has much money. 9. He has a lot of money.	16. Tom has hamburger for lunch. 17. Chan-ho has Kim-bap for lunch. 18. He has Bulgogi for lunch.

NOTE

* have와 has의 용법

(1) have: I와 you, we, they 즉 주어가 1인칭, 2인칭, 3인칭 복수인 경우
(2) has: he 나 she 즉 주어가 3인칭 단수의 경우

* many와 much의 용법

(1) many: 셀 수 있는 명사 앞에
(2) much: 셀 수 없는 명사 앞에

예 I have many books. I have much water.
You have many books. You have much water.
He has many books. He has much water.

다음 그림을 보고 단어를 영어로 써 보세요.

1.	2.	3.	4.
5.	6.	7.	8.

다음 문장을 영어로 말해 보세요. (영어로 읽기 소요시간:)

1. 나는 책을 가지고 있다.
   나는 많은 책을 가지고 있다.

2. 당신은 물을 가지고 있다.
   당신은 많은 물을 가지고 있다.

3. 그는 이야기책을 가지고 있다.
   그는 많은 이야기책을 가지고 있다.

4. 그녀는 친구가 있다.
   그녀는 두 친구가 있다.

5. 존은 아침 7시에 아침을 먹는다.
   메리는 12시에 점심을 먹는다.

6. 나는 저녁 7시에 저녁을 먹는다.
   그는 저녁 8시에 저녁을 먹는다.

LESSON 16 (SIXTEEN)

I GET UP AT SIX.

	I get up. I get up at six.
	I sleep. I sleep at ten.
	I go. I go to school.
	I come. I come home.
	I study. I study at school.
	I play. I play at home.

NEW WORDS

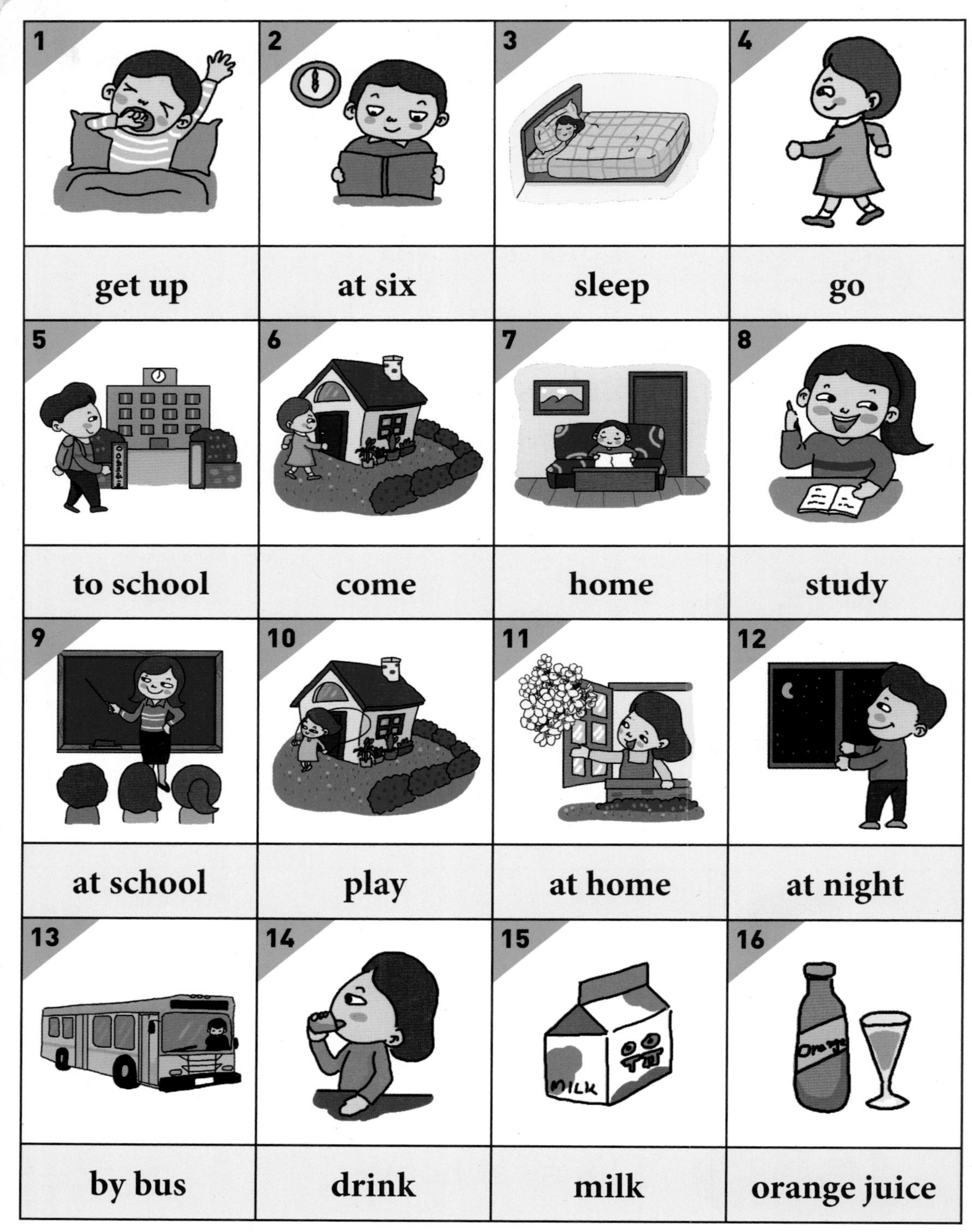
1
get up
2
at six
3
sleep
4
go
5
to school
6
come
7
home
8
study
9
at school
10
play
11
at home
12
at night
13
by bus
14
drink
15
milk
MILK
16
orange juice
Orange

PATTERN PRACTICE

[I get up ______________.] 의 문형

1. I get up. 2. I get up at six. 3. I get up at six every morning.	10. I come. 11. I come home. 12. I come home at five.
4. I sleep. 5. I sleep at ten. 6. I sleep at ten at night.	13. I study. 14. I study English. 15. I study English at school.
7. I go. 8. I go to school. 9. I go to school by bus.	16. I drink. 17. I drink milk. 18. I drink orange juice.

NOTE

* 인칭의 용법

(1) 1인칭: 말하는 사람 즉 I, 그리고 나를 포함한 we

(2) 2인칭: 말을 듣는 사람 즉 you

(3) 3인칭: 1인칭과 2인칭을 뺀 제 3자, 이 세상의 모든 것 즉 he, she, this, ……
자기자신의 이름도 3인칭에 속한다.

* 일반동사는 주어가 3인칭 단수의 경우 동사 뒤에 s나 es를 붙인다.

예 I play.
You play.
He plays.

다음 그림을 보고 단어를 영어로 써 보세요.

1.	2.	3.	4.
5.	6.	7.	8.

다음 문장을 영어로 말해 보세요. (영어로 읽기 소요시간:)

1. 나는 일어난다.
   나는 6시에 일어난다.

2. 나는 잔다.
   나는 10시에 잔다.

3. 나는 간다.
   나는 학교에 간다.

4. 나는 온다.
   나는 집에 온다.

5. 나는 공부한다.
   나는 학교에서 공부한다.

6. 나는 논다
   나는 집에서 논다.

LESSON 17 (SEVENTEEN)

YOU READ A BOOK.

	You read a book. You read an English book.
	You write a letter. You write a letter in English.
	You teach English. You teach Korean.
	You learn English. You learn Korean.
	You brush your teeth. You brush your teeth before breakfast.
	You wash your face. You wash your face and hands.

NEW WORDS

1	2	3	4
read	write	letter	in English
5	6	7	8
teach	learn	brush	teeth
9	10	11	12
before	wash	face	hand
13	14	15	16
fast	slowly	diary	bathroom

PATTERN PRACTICE

[You read ______________.]의 문형

1. You read a book. 2. You read an English book. 3. You read an English book fast.	10. You learn English. 11. You learn Korean. 12. You learn Korean at home.
4. You write a diary. 5. You write a diary in Korean. 6. You write a diary in Korean slowly.	13. You brush your teeth. 14. You brush your teeth at six. 15. You brush your teeth before breakfast.
7. You teach English. 8. You teach Korean. 9. You teach French at school.	16. You wash your face. 17. You wash your face and hands. 18. You wash your face and hands in the bathroom.

NOTE

* 동사 뒤에 s를 붙이는 예

(1) play …… plays
(2) sleep …… sleeps
(3) come …… comes

* 동사 뒤에 es를 붙이는 예

(4) go …… goes
(5) brush …… brushes
(6) study …… studies

* 동사 활용의 비교

I am a pupil.	I have a pencil.	I play baseball.
You are a pupil.	You have a pencil.	You play baseball.
She is a pupil.	She has a pencil.	She plays baseball.

다음 그림을 보고 단어를 영어로 써 보세요.

다음 문장을 영어로 말해 보세요. (영어로 읽기 소요시간:)

1. 당신은 책을 읽는다.
   당신은 영어책을 읽는다.

2. 당신은 편지를 쓴다.
   당신은 영어로 편지를 쓴다.

3. 당신은 영어를 가르친다.
   당신은 한국어를 가르친다.

4. 당신은 영어를 배운다.
   당신은 한국어를 배운다.

5. 당신은 이를 닦는다.
   당신은 아침식사 전에 이를 닦는다.

6. 당신은 얼굴을 씻는다.
   당신은 얼굴과 손을 씻는다.

LESSON 18 (EIGHTEEN)

HE WALKS SLOWLY.

	He walks. He walks slowly.
	He runs. He runs fast.
	She swims. She swims well.
	She skates. She skates very well.
	Tom laughs. Tom laughs big.
	Jane smiles. Jane smiles brightly.

NEW WORDS

1	2	3	4
walk	run	swim	skate
5	**6**	**7**	**8**
very	well	laugh	big
9	**10**	**11**	**12**
smile	brightly	sea	ice
13	**14**	**15**	**16**
cry	road	shout	jungle

[He walks ______________.] 의 문형

1. He walks. 2. He walks slowly. 3. He walks to school slowly.	10. She skates. 11. She skates well. 12. She skates well on the ice.
4. He runs. 5. He runs fast. 6. He runs home fast.	13. Tom cries. 14. Tom cries out. 15. Tom cries out on the road.
7. She swims. 8. She swims well. 9. She swims well in the sea.	16. Jane shouts. 17. Jane shouts out. 18. Jane shouts out in the jungle.

NOTE

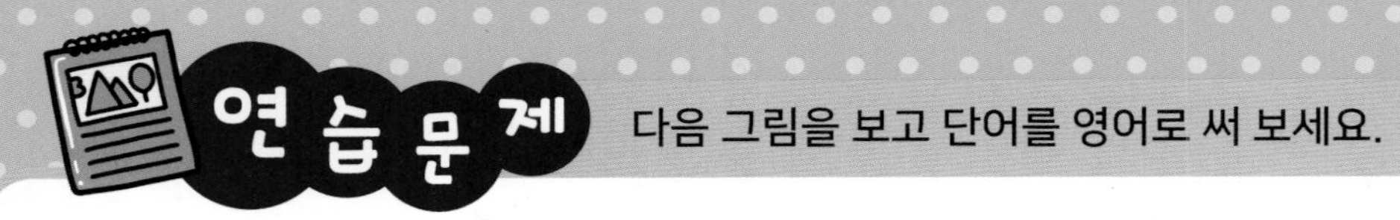

다음 그림을 보고 단어를 영어로 써 보세요.

1.	2.	3.	4.
5.	6.	7.	8.

다음 문장을 영어로 말해 보세요. (영어로 읽기 소요시간:)

1. 그는 걷는다.
   그는 천천히 걷는다.

2. 그는 달린다.
   그는 빨리 달린다.

3. 그녀는 수영한다.
   그녀는 수영을 잘한다.

4. 그녀는 스케이트를 탄다.
   그녀는 스케이트를 매우 잘 탄다.

5. 탐은 웃는다.
   탐은 크게 웃는다.

6. 제인은 미소를 짓는다.
   제인은 미소를 밝게 짓는다.

LESSON 19 (NINETEEN)

I DON'T HAVE A BOOK.

I have a book.
I don't have a notebook.

You have a bag.
You don't have a handbag.

He has lunch at noon.
She doesn't have lunch at noon.

I wake up early.
I don't wake up late.

You go to bed early.
You don't go to bed late.

He goes to church on Sunday.
She doesn't go to church on Monday.

NEW WORDS

1	2	3	4
notebook	bag	handbag	wake up
5	**6**	**7**	**8**
early	late	go to bed	church
9	**10**	**11**	**12**
on Sunday	key	knife	ring
13	**14**	**15**	**16**
a cup of	coffee	a glass of	tomato juice

PATTERN PRACTICE

[I don't have ______________.]의 문형

1. I have a key. 2. I don't have a key.	9. Tom has lunch at noon. 10. Jane doesn't have lunch at noon.
3. You have a knife. 4. You don't have a knife.	11. I go to school by bus. 12. I don't go to school by car.
5. He has a ring. 6. He doesn't have a ring.	13. He drinks a cup of coffee. 14. He doesn't drink much coffee.
7. She has two cousins. 8. She doesn't have two cousins.	15. She drinks a glass of juice. 16. She doesn't drink much juice.

NOTE

* have동사의 부정문 만드는 방법

동사 앞에 don't나 doesn't를 써 넣는다.
이때 주의할 점은 has를 have로 바꾸어 준다.

don't: have가 올 때
doesn't: has가 올 때

* 일반동사의 부정문은 have동사의 부정문 만드는 법과 같다.

예 I have a book. I don't have a book.	He has a book. He doesn't have a book.
I play baseball. I don't play baseball.	He plays baseball. He doesn't play baseball.

다음 그림을 보고 단어를 영어로 써 보세요.

1.	2.	3.	4.
5.	6.	7.	8.

다음 문장을 영어로 말해 보세요. (영어로 읽기 소요시간:　　)

1. 나는 책을 가지고 있다.
   나는 공책을 가지고 있지 않다.

2. 당신은 가방을 가지고 있다.
   당신은 손가방을 가지고 있지 않다.

3. 그는 점심을 정오에 먹는다.
   그녀는 점심을 정오에 먹지 않는다.

4. 나는 일찍 일어난다.
   나는 늦게 일어나지 않는다.

5. 당신은 일찍 잠자리에 든다.
   당신은 늦게 잠자리에 들지 않는다.

LESSON 20 (TWENTY)

DO YOU HAVE A CAP?

	Do you have a cap? Yes, I do.
	Do you have a hat? No, I don't. I have a cap.
	Does he have a watch? Yes, he does.
	Does she have a rose? No, she doesn't. She has a lily.
	Does your sister have a tulip? Yes, she has a tulip.
	Do they have many sunflowers? No, they don't. They have some sunflowers.

NEW WORDS

1	2	3	4
cap	hat	watch	rose
5	6	7	8
lily	tulip	sunflower	sweater
9	10	11	12
blouse	skirt	shoes	stockings
13	14	15	16
doll	twenty two	twenty three	twenty four

[Do you have ___________?]의 문형

1. Do you have a sweater? 2. Yes, I do. 3. Yes, I have a sweater.	10. Does he have shoes? 11. No, he doesn't. 12. No, he doesn't have shoes.
4. Do you have a blouse? 5. No, I don't. 6. No, I don't have a blouse.	13. Does Jane have stockings? 14. Yes, she does. 15. Yes, she has stockings.
7. Does she have a skirt? 8. Yes, she does. 9. Yes, she has a skirt.	16. Does your sister have a doll? 17. No, she doesn't. 18. No, she doesn't have a doll.

NOTE

* have동사의 의문문 만드는 방법

문장 앞에 Do나 Does를 써 넣는다. 이 때 has는 have로 바꾸어 준다.

Do: have가 올 때

Does: has가 올 때

* 일반동사의 의문문도 have동사의 의문문과 같다.

예 You have a book.
Do you have a book?

He has a book.
Does he have a book?

I play baseball.
Do I play baseball?

He plays baseball.
Does he play baseball?

다음 그림을 보고 단어를 영어로 써 보세요.

1.	2.	3.	4.
5.	6.	7.	8.

다음 문장을 영어로 말해 보세요. (영어로 읽기 소요시간:)

1. 당신은 모자를 가지고 있습니까?
   예, 그렇습니다.

2. 당신은 중절모를 가지고 있습니까?
   아니요, 그렇지 않습니다.

3. 그는 시계를 가지고 있습니까?
   예, 그렇습니다.

4. 그녀는 장미를 가지고 있습니까?
   아니요, 그렇지 않습니다.
   그녀는 백합을 가지고 있습니다.

5. 당신의 여동생은 튤립을 가지고 있습니까?
   예, 그녀는 튤립을 가지고 있습니다.

6. 그들은 많은 해바라기 꽃들을 가지고 있습니까?
   아니요, 그렇지 않습니다.
   그들은 약간의 해바라기 꽃들을 가지고 있습니다.

LESSON 21 (TWENTY ONE)

DO YOU DRINK WATER?

	Do you drink water? Yes, I do.
	Do you drink milk every morning? No, I don't. I drink milk sometimes.
	Does he brush his teeth in the morning? Yes, he does.
	Does Tom go to school by bus? No, he doesn't. He walks to school.
	Does Jack play baseball after school? Yes, he does.
	Does Mary play the piano? No, she doesn't. She plays the violin.

NEW WORDS

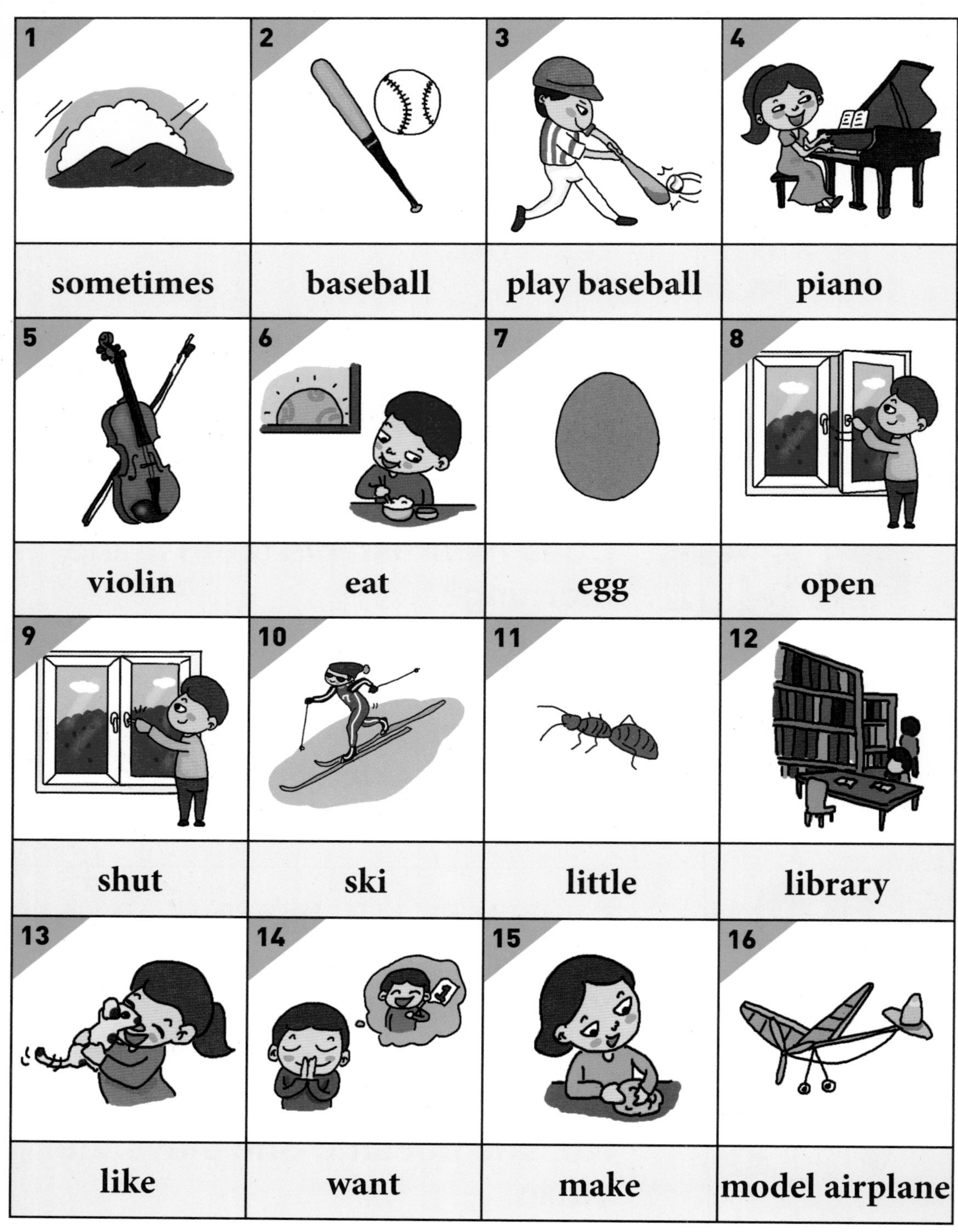
1
sometimes
2
baseball
3
play baseball
4
piano
5
violin
6
eat
7
egg
8
open
9
shut
10
ski
11
little
12
library
13
like
14
want
15
make
16
model airplane

[Do you ________ ___?]의 문형

1. Do you eat an egg? 2. Yes, I do.	9. Do you go to the library? 10. Yes, I go to the library.
3. Do you open the door? 4. No, I don't. I shut the door.	11. Do you like him? 12. Yes, I like him.
5. Does he skate in winter? 6. No, he doesn't. He skis in winter.	13. Does he want an English book? 14. No, he doesn't.
7. Does your sister cry? 8. Yes, she cries sometimes.	15. Do you make a model airplane? 16. No, I don't make it.

NOTE

* 기수와 서수

(1) 기수

one	eleven
two	twelve
three	thirteen
four	fourteen
five	fifteen
six	sixteen
seven	seventeen
eight	eighteen
nine	nineteen
ten	twenty

(2) 서수

first(1st)	eleventh(11th)
second(2nd)	twelfth(12th)
third(3rd)	thirteenth(13th)
fourth(4th)	fourteenth(14th)
fifth(5th)	fifteenth(15th)
sixth(6th)	sixteenth(16th)
seventh(7th)	seventeenth(17th)
eighth(8th)	eighteenth(18th)
ninth(9th)	nineteenth(19th)
tenth(10th)	twentieth(20th)

다음 그림을 보고 단어를 영어로 써 보세요.

1.	2.	3.	4.
5.	6.	7.	8.

다음 문장을 영어로 말해 보세요. (영어로 읽기 소요시간:)

1. 당신은 물을 마십니까?
   예, 그렇습니다.

2. 당신은 매일 아침 우유를 마십니까?
   아니요, 그렇지 않습니다.
   나는 때때로 우유를 마십니다.

3. 그는 아침에 이를 닦습니까?
   예, 그렇습니다.

4. 탐은 버스로 학교에 갑니까?
   아니요, 그렇지 않습니다.
   그는 학교에 걸어갑니다.

5. 잭은 방과 후 야구를 합니까?
   예, 그렇습니다.

6. 메리는 피아노를 칩니까?
   아니요, 그렇지 않습니다.
   그녀는 바이올린을 연주합니다.

LESSON 22 (TWENTY TWO)

WHAT TIME IS IT?

	What time is it? It is seven o'clock.
	What time is it now? It is six-thirty.
	What time is it now? It is half past six.
	What day is it today? It is Sunday today.
	What is the date today? It is September 16th.
 	When is your birthday? My birthday is September 16th.

NEW WORDS

1	2	3	4
time	o'clock	now	six-thirty
5	**6**	**7**	**8**
half	past	day	February
9	**10**	**11**	**12**
date	when	birthday	Monday
13	**14**	**15**	**16**
January	March	May	Tuesday

PATTERN PRACTICE

[What time is it ?]의 문형

1. What time is it? 2. It is six o'clock.	9. What is the date today? 10. It is January 27th.
3. What time is it now? 4. It is six thirty.	11. When is your birthday? 12. My birthday is March 25th.
5. What time is it now? 6. It is half past six.	13. What's the date today? 14. It's May 5th.
7. What day is it today? 8. It is Monday today.	15. What day is it today? 16. It's Tuesday today.

NOTE

* 요일

Sunday: 일요일

Monday: 월요일

Tuesday: 화요일

Wednesday: 수요일

Thursday: 목요일

Friday: 금요일

Saturday: 토요일

* 월

January: 1월

February: 2월

March: 3월

April: 4월

May: 5월

June: 6월

July: 7월

August: 8월

September: 9월

October: 10월

November: 11월

December: 12월

연습문제

다음 그림을 보고 단어를 영어로 써 보세요.

Monday 7月 20日	Tuesday 9月 16日	지금 부터야!	
1.	2.	3.	4.
언제			half
5.	6.	7.	8.

다음 문장을 영어로 말해 보세요. (영어로 읽기 소요시간:)

1. 몇 시 입니까?
   7시 입니다.

2. 지금은 몇 시 입니까?
   6시 30분입니다.

3. 지금은 몇 시 입니까?
   6시 반입니다.

4. 오늘은 무슨 요일입니까?
   오늘은 일요일입니다.

5. 오늘은 몇 일 입니까?
   9월 16일입니다.

6. 당신의 생일은 언제 입니까?
   나의 생일은 9월 16일입니다.

LESSON 23 (TWENTY THREE)

THERE IS A BOOK ON THE DESK.

	There is a book on the desk. There are books on the desk.
	There are some flowers in the garden. There are many trees in the garden.
	Are there many balls in the basket? Yes, there are.
	Is there much water in the pool? No, there isn't.
	How many seasons are there in a year? There are four seasons in a year.
	Here is a hospital. Here are many buildings.

NEW WORDS

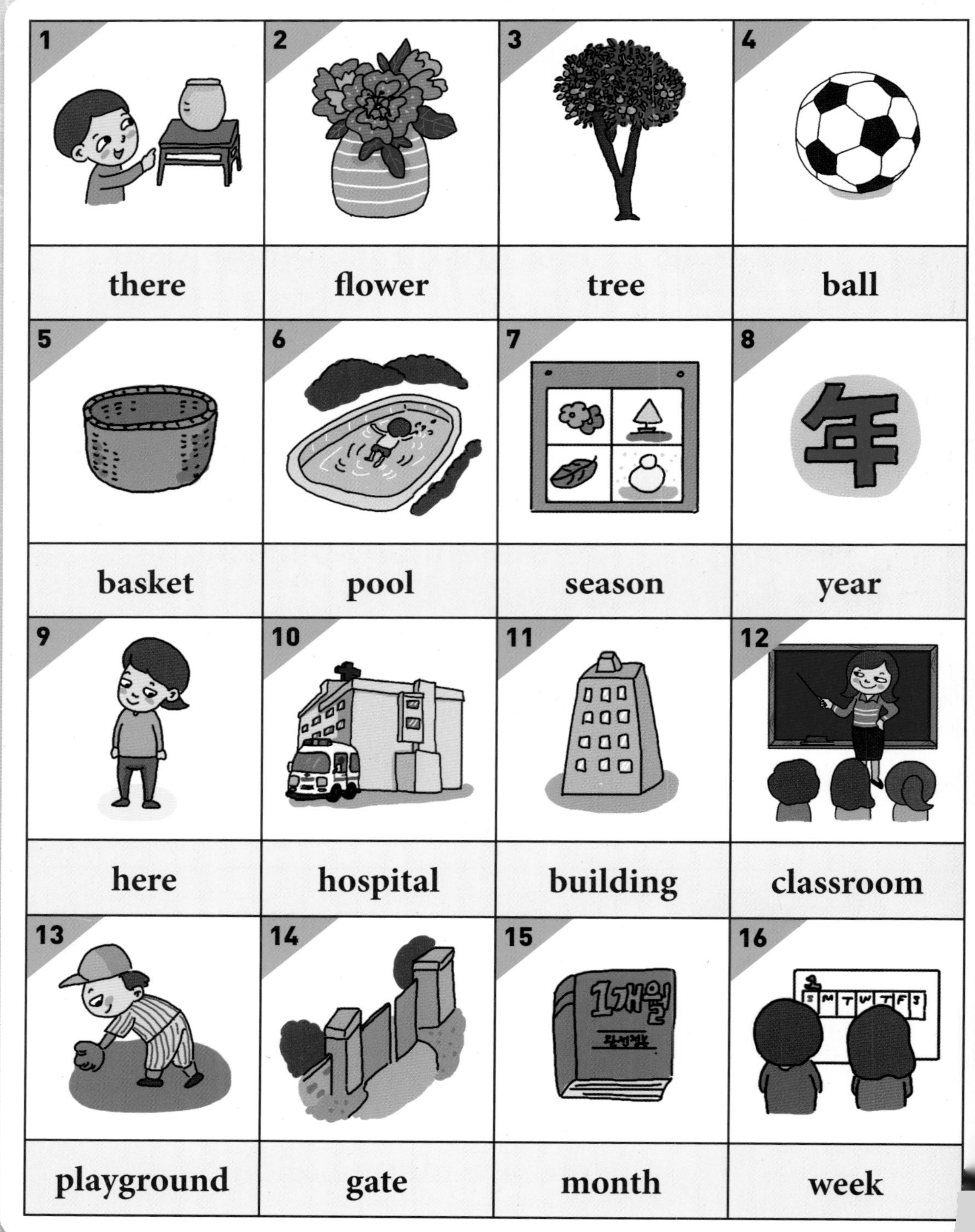

1 there
2 flower
3 tree
4 ball
5 basket
6 pool
7 season
8 year
年
9 here
10 hospital
11 building
12 classroom
13 playground
14 gate
15 month
1개월
16 week

[There is ______________ .]의 문형

1. There is a pen on the desk. 2. There are two pens on the desk.	9. Are there boys on the playground? 10. Yes, there are.
3. There are some pens on the desk. 4. There is some milk in a glass.	11. How many months are there in a year? 12. There are twelve months in it.
5. Is there a dog at the gate? 6. No, there isn't.	13. How many days are there in a week? 14. There are seven days in it.
7. Are there students in the class? 8. Yes, there are.	15. Here is a lunch box. 16. Here is not a lunch box.

NOTE

[There is + 단수명사………….]: …………이 있습니다.
[There are + 복수명사………….]: …………들이 있습니다.

예 There is a book on the desk.
There are books on the desk.

There is not a book on the desk.
There are not books on the desk.

Is there a book on the desk?
Are there books on the desk?

(주의) (1) [There is …… .]의 문장에서 there는 해석하지 않는다.
(2) [There is …… .]의 해석은 문장 뒤에서부터 시작한다.

다음 그림을 보고 단어를 영어로 써 보세요.

1.	2.	3.	4.
5.	6.	7.	8.

다음 문장을 영어로 말해 보세요. (영어로 읽기 소요시간:)

1. 책상 위에 책이 있습니다.
   책상 위에 책들이 있습니다.

2. 정원에는 약간의 꽃들이 있습니다.
   정원에는 많은 나무들이 있습니다.

3. 바구니에 많은 공들이 있습니까?
   예, 있습니다.

4. 풀장 안에는 많은 물이 있습니까?
   아니요, 없습니다.

5. 1년에는 몇 계절이 있습니까?
   1년에는 4계절이 있습니다.

6. 여기에 병원이 있습니다.
   여기에 많은 건물들이 있습니다.

LESSON 24 (TWENTY FOUR)

STAND UP, PLEASE.

	Stand up, please. Don't sit down.
	Please sit down. Don't stand up.
	Wake up early. Don't sleep late.
	Let's sing a song together. Let's not go out at night.
	Let's play baseball after school. Let's not play on the road.
	Let's study hard. Let's not watch TV too long.

NEW WORDS

1	2	3	4
stand up	sit down	please	hard
5	6	7	8
Let's	sing	song	together
9	10	11	12
look at	come in	close	go on a picnic
13	14	15	16
help	make a noise	mouth	hurry

PATTERN PRACTICE

[Stand up.]의 문형

1. Look at me. 2. Don't look at me.	9. Let's go on a picnic. 10. Let's not go on a picnic.
3. Look at the blackboard. 4. Don't look at the blackboard.	11. Please help me. 12. Don't help him.
5. Come in, please. 6. Don't come in.	13. Please come on in. 14. Don't make a noise.
7. Open your book. 8. Close your book.	15. Shut your mouth. 16. Don't hurry.

NOTE

(1) Go home.
Don't go home.

Be kind.
Don't be kind.

Go home, please.
Don't go home, please.

Please be kind.
Please don't be kind.

(2) Let's go home.
Let's not go home.

Let us go home.
Let us not go home.

Let me go home.
Let me not go home.

Let him go home.
Let him not go home.

1.	2.	3.	4.
5.	6.	7.	8.

다음 문장을 영어로 말해 보세요. (영어로 읽기 소요시간:)

1. 일어나세요.
   앉지 마세요.

2. 앉으세요.
   일어나지 마세요.

3. 일찍 일어나세요.
   늦게 자지 마세요.

4. 다 같이 노래합시다.
   밤에 밖으로 나가지 맙시다.

5. 방과 후 야구를 합시다.
   길 위에서 놀지 맙시다.

6. 열심히 공부합시다.
   너무 오래 TV를 보지 맙시다.